YOUR KNOWLEDGE HAS VALUE

IoT Applications in Smart Grids Using Edge Computing

Brinda Patel
Jigar Sarda
Amit Thakkar
Arpita Patel

Bibliographic information published by the German National Library:

The German National Library lists this publication in the National Bibliography; detailed bibliographic data are available on the Internet at http://dnb.dnb.de.

ISBN: 9783389079201
This book is also available as an ebook.

© GRIN Publishing GmbH
Trappentreustraße 1
80339 München

Print and binding: Books on Demand GmbH, Norderstedt, Germany
Printed on acid-free paper from responsible sources.

The present work has been carefully prepared. Nevertheless, authors and publishers do not incur liability for the correctness of information, notes, links and advice as well as any printing errors.

GRIN web shop: https://www.grin.com/document/1499929

IoT Applications in Smart Grids Using Edge Computing

Abstract

Smart Grid integrates renewable and green technology into the traditional electrical infrastructure. Smart embedded gadgets with sophisticated decision-making capabilities will boost Smart Grid's efficiency. Energy industry has seen a transformation because of the incorporation of Internet of Things technology in Smart Grids. Edge Computing is applied to enhance efficiency and reliability of Smart Grid operations. A complete ecosystem for smart cities is created when digital platforms, edge computing, and IoT solutions are combined. They make it possible for massive amounts of data to be gathered, processed, and analysed, enabling city officials, businesses, and citizens to make wise decisions and promote innovation. In conclusion, a convincing paradigm for addressing the changing issues in the energy industry is presented by the combination of IoT and Edge Computing in Smart Grids. The suggested framework opens the door for creative solutions that support a more resilient and sustainable energy infrastructure in addition to enhancing the capabilities of currently available Smart Grid applications.

1. INTRODUCTION

1.1 Overview of Internet of Things (IoT)

The IoT is a system where non-living items autonomously gather and share data over wireless networks. They may also be defined as the process of linking different devices and items, such as smart TVs. Smart sensors provide a novel kind of communication between items and people. The IoT is a widely used word in contemporary society. The IoT refers to the proliferation and development of internet-connected networks. It is an extensive network created by linking numerous devices that possess information, enabling people, machines, and things to connect at any time and location. The IoT is a very beneficial kind of wireless connectivity in the 21st century. Currently, IoT technology is significantly impacting people's lives, enhancing convenience and simplifying daily tasks. The IoT is significantly influencing this sector and is emerging as a major catalyst for innovation and success. IoT devices have gained significance due to their fast growth in recent years. As we can see in figure 1, all gadgets in the IoT ecosystem may be linked to the internet, and the IoTs has rapidly and significantly infiltrated numerous industries. Over the next ten years, the impact and rate of integration of IoT technologies will increase. The impact and rate of integration of IoT technologies will be substantial [1].

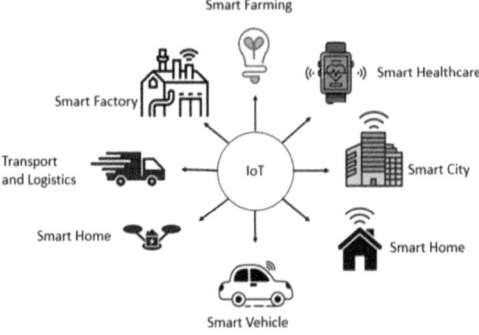

Figure 1 Applications of IoT- "Author's own work"

IoT is a network capable of transmitting data to a computer for human analysis. Various technologies are used to monitor and regulate vital infrastructure and communications for crucial tasks. Furthermore, the semantic-oriented concept encompasses several applications that make use of intelligent devices. IoT technology has become more important in recent years. IoT items are versatile devices equipped with transceivers, protocol stacks, and microcontrollers. Facilitating communication between IoT devices and other organizations allows for the creation of completely automated systems [1]. The architecture IoT is made up of many interconnected devices that use sensing, communication, networking, and information processing technologies [3-5]. These devices possess advanced sensing, computation, and communication capabilities that enable them to communicate, detect, or interact with their internal state or external surroundings [6-7]. IoT systems provide the next ground-breaking idea in evolving the internet into a comprehensive network that facilitates seamless communication across societies, people, and intelligent devices [8-9]. Advancements in technologies like wireless sensor networks (WSN), radiofrequency identification (RFID), and Micro-Electro Mechanical Systems (MEMS) are enhancing the capabilities of the IoT to access and use information. Simultaneously, enhancing production efficiency, elevating product quality, lowering product prices and resource consumption, and delivering more transparent and personalized services to consumers [2]. IoT technology, a prominent area of technology, is increasingly being used in several domains [3].

1.2 Overview of Smart Grid

Enhancing the generation, distribution, and transmission of electricity is possible with the help of smart grid technology.9 Its adaptability allows for easier installation and requires less space than typical grids. The Smart grid design concept focuses on achieving grid observability, enhancing asset controllability, improving power system performance and security, and optimizing the economic elements of operations, maintenance, and planning [60]. Smart grid technology may be used at the micro-grid level and interconnected with other micro-grids to create a comprehensive Smart grid network. Smart grids offer significant potential to enhance the dependability of electricity transmission and distribution in poor nations with inadequate infrastructure. In the US, transportation emits 20% of all carbon dioxide, whereas energy production emits 40%. This is a result of the significant increase in the demand for power. Smart grids are being seen as crucial for efficiently distributing electric power and eventually reducing greenhouse gases and pollutants such as NOx and SOx [61]. It will assist the client in predicting their demand and optimizing the cost-effective use of energy. The smart grid does not have a defined beginning. This notion began to evolve with the inception of electrical network distribution systems. Various needs such as regulation, monitoring, pricing, and services for the transmission and distribution of electrical power have emerged. Typically, smart grid adoption involves installing smart meters. However, the primary concern that remains unresolved despite technological progress is the dependability and efficiency of energy transmission and distribution via the electric power grid.

1.3 Overview of Edge Computing (EC)

IoT devices are producing a vast quantity of data, although their resources are constrained. Hence, the duties of the application running on IoT devices should be transferred to faraway cloud data centers. Offloading every jobs to the cloud places a substantial strain on the network. Edge computing may be able to help with this problem. Computation offloading, as defined by earlier research [12–15], is an optimisation issue that aims to reduce offloading expenses while preserving performance guarantees. Cloud computing (CC) resources are situated in remote data centers, leading to significant issues with communication latency and network bandwidth. EC is preferable to cloud for growing IoT applications because to the proximity of computing resources to the user. The study focuses on the incorporation of EC into IoT-based smart grid systems. Analysed is the framework for EC-IoT-based smart grids, along with the essential requirements needed to establish the EC-IoT-based smart grid system. Identified are major concerns and obstacles encountered in implementing EC-IoT-based SG systems [7]. CC cannot provide low-latency applications because to the significant transmission distances and the expensive construction costs, especially when dealing with massive amounts of real-time data [8]. In EC, devices are placed in close proximity to the user or the data source, but in cloud computing, tasks are carried out within cloud environments. Applications are hosted close to end users, either on-site or in smaller edge data centres, as part of EC, a component of CC.

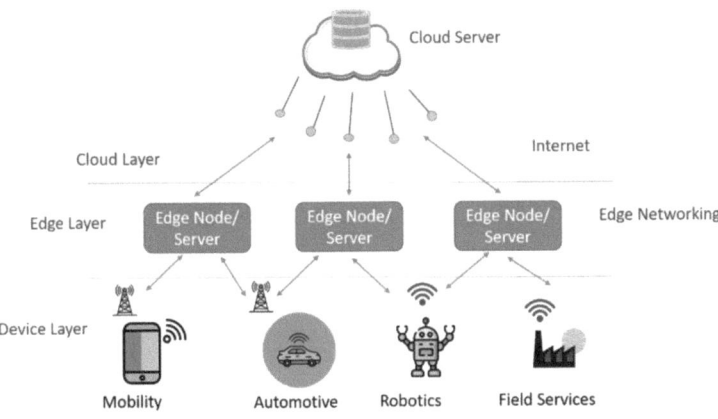

Figure 2 Edge Computing Architecture- "Author's own work"

Unlike CC, EC has a complicated architecture where handling, storing, and networking duties are performed at the major data centre as well as at the user's location which is shown in figure 2. With CC's two-layer architecture, all processing takes place at the central data centre. A suggested CC reference design was proposed in [9]. CC provides a centralized center for processing and storing data, causing delays in data retrieval, unlike EC. Figure 3 illustrates the technical and over-all dissimilarities between EC and CC. The notion of IoT-based smart grid increases the operations, administration, and maintenance of smart grids, making it essential for grid growth.

Parameters	Edge Computing	Cloud Computing
Locality of application	Local	Global
Authentication	High	Low
Access to networks	LAN or WLAN	LAN or WLAN
Accessibility	Highly redundant	High
Content producer	Humans, Sensors and devices	Mostly humans
Producing content	Anywhere	Central
Delay	Low	High
Control method	Distributed	Centralized
Mobility Assistance	Supported	Limited
Usage of Services	At the edge	Centralized
Between client and server distance	One or several hops	Several hops
Server nodes	Very large	Few

Figure 3 EC and CC Comparison- "Author's own work"

At the edge, we have to provide strong processing system and better storage capacity for the wireless access network. Edge Computing is thought to offer major advantages over cloud computing in smart grids. Due to its convenience and efficiency, wireless communication is often used in smart grid networks [16]. The standard smart grid communication network design consists of three layers: wide area network (WAN), home area network (HAN), and neighbourhood area network (NAN).

The smart meters in the HAN monitor the energy consumption status and send the data to the gateway in the NAN. Figure 4 illustrates the structure of smart grid networks using EC. The EC servers may be located at the gateways. EC servers may be used by smart meters to do calculation activities with the help of EC. The Smart Grid network system which is based on EC paradigm propose a distinct provision environment known for its reduced latency, dependability, and cost-effectiveness compared to cloud computing servers in faraway data centres [17].

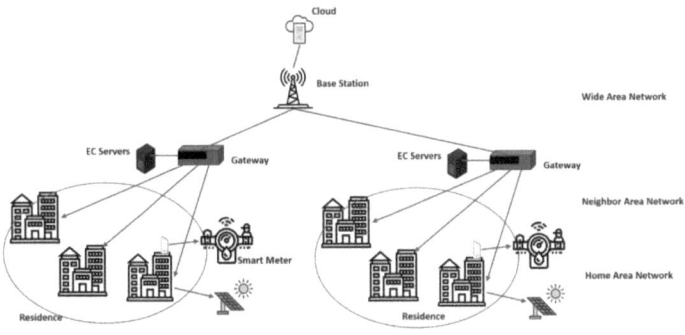

Figure 4 EC based framework of smart grid- "Author's own work"

2. Smart Grid

For years, our residences, businesses, and factories have relied on the traditional electrical system for electricity. However, as technology advances and energy needs change, there is an increasing need for a more durable, dependable, and efficient energy distribution infrastructure. Here is where the concept of a "smart grid" becomes beneficial. A smart grid optimizes electricity generation, distribution, and consumption by using control technologies and modern computer. It is a development of the traditional grid system into a digitally enabled network that enables bidirectional and immediate data exchange and communication between grid operators, power providers, and customers [8].

2.1 Smart Grid Essentials:

Some of the key features of SG is listed below [8]:

1. Advanced Metering Infrastructure (AMI) involves the installation of smart meters that enable users to observe their energy consumption in instantaneous time, a key feature of smart grids. These meters provide bidirectional communication between utilities and consumers, enhancing demand response and billing precision.

2. Distributed Energy Resources (DERs): Smart grids have the capability to establish connections between different energy sources like wind turbines, solar panels and energy storage devices. These dispersed power sources could contribute to the grid's energy balance by supplying energy.

3. Automatic Monitoring and Control: It use sensors and automation to continuously monitor grid status. Grid operators may enhance reliability and minimize downtime by

promptly identifying and addressing disruptions, faults, or variations utilising data from the present.

4. Load Management and Request Response: Consumers may actively participate in demand response programs using smart grid capabilities. By encouraging users to adjust their energy consumption during peak hours or in response to system limitations, these initiatives contribute to increased grid efficiency and decreased grid stress.

5. Increase Grid Efficiency: Reducing energy losses during the transmission and distribution of electricity is the goal of smart grids. Optimising the power flow and increasing its responsiveness to consumer demand can improve the overall efficiency of the grid.

6. Enhanced Grid Security: To protect against intrusions and keep the electricity supply dependable, smart grids require robust cybersecurity protocols.

Traditional power grids consist of a vast network of loosely connected synchronous alternating current networks. Electricity is produced by various power facilities such as diesel-fired plants, coal-fired, hydroelectric, and nuclear. Subsequently, the generated power is transmitted to distant load centres using high-voltage transmission lines. At the distribution end, electrical distribution systems deliver power to consumers at a lower voltage. A centralised system is used to monitor and manage each grid in order to ensure that the energy produced by power plants meets consumer demands and does not exceed the capacity of the power plants. Utility businesses handle the functions of generating, transmitting, and distributing electrical power to users. They employ a billing process to recoup expenses and make a profit. Electrical energy use has significantly risen since 1970 [18]. A significant amount of energy is lost due to ineffective customer appliances, lack of technologies, inconsistent monitoring, communication issues, and inadequate energy storage systems [19]. Currently, electricity networks are encountering issues such as security, dependability, increasing renewable energy sources, and escalating energy consumption. SG takes crucial choices based on energy requirements, such as power utilization, real-time pricing, self-healing and scheduling electrical energy consumption. These choices may enhance the electricity quality and efficiency of the system. Implementing distributed automation in the SG is necessary to accomplish these goals. Currently, electrical power is the foundation of all contemporary technology. The projection states that global power consumption will rise by 70% over the next three decades, from 25 to 42 thousand terawatt-hours by 2050. According to Figure 5, renewable energy sources are expected to account for around 56% of all electricity generated globally. [20]. As science and technology advance, power is generated from several sources. The power grids are interconnected in a synchronized and seamless manner to efficiently regulate, monitor, and transfer electricity while reducing power usage [21]. To make sure that the electricity produced by the plant satisfies consumer demand and stays within the power plant's capacity, every electricity grid is observed and managed by means of a centralised management system. Utility providers use production, transmission, and distribution operations to offer electrical energy to customers. This is done via a payment mechanism designed to cover expenses and generate profits. Electric energy consumption prices have risen notably from 2.6 to 13.19 US cents per kWh between 1960 and 2021 [21]. Currently, a significant quantity of power is squandered because of ineffective customer gadgets, the absence of monitoring, communication, and smart technology, as well as storage systems [22]. Additionally, the variety of RESs, security and privacy concerns, dependability challenges, and an increasing need for energy usage are all plaguing today's grids. The smart grid is an ideal approach for addressing these difficulties. Smart grids employ a variety of IoT devices, smart sensors, and terminals, such as temperature, vibration, humidity, video, and current leak sensors. The IoT-based Smart Grids consist of six key features: communication protocols, SDN objects, smart sensors, emphasis on information security and privacy, cost-effectiveness, and data analytics using fog, edge, and cloud computing technologies. The recognition of cloud computing's efficacy in grid management applications has been shown in recent decades [23]. The fast growth of IoT devices is leading to a significant rise in data volume, resulting in higher computational expenses and longer service response times [24]. Hence, new models and methodologies are necessary for processing, calculating, and storing this data. EC has recently emerged as a viable approach to address these issues. The European Commission enables the proximity of cloud capabilities to end-users, leading to decreased computing costs and faster service response times. Edge computing is the essential technology for achieving immediate reaction times in IoT-based smart grids [25].

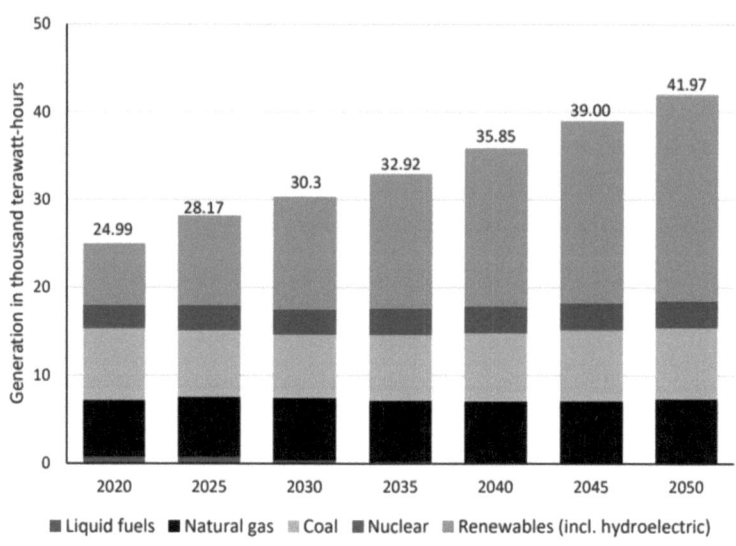

Figure 5 Electricity consumption forecast for the period of 2020 to 2050 [38]

3. Understanding IoT in Smart Grids

IoT technology is becoming more and more important. IoT refers to a networked device that can communicate and share data, which can then be analyze by people on a computer. Billions of smart devices are integrated into complex networks to provide dynamic functionality such as keeping an eye on and overseeing vital communications and infrastructure [26]. Three key concepts underpin the Internet of Things: things, semantics, and the internet. Things-oriented ideas make use of a variety of smart devices, including cameras, laser scanners, sensors, actuators, RFID tags, and GPS. The internet-oriented idea facilitates connectivity among smart devices using various communication technologies such as Zig Bee, Bluetooth and WiFi. The semantic-oriented notion encompasses several applications with the help of intelligent gadgets. The IoT links many networked gadgets used in everyday life to the Internet. Multiple sectors such as healthcare, transportation, security surveillance, agriculture, power grids, household appliances, and military have been automated using IoT technology [27]. Literature studies have extensively covered several aspects of IoT, including architectural features, permissive technologies, implementation, and open issues [28-30]. Studies on the IoT's wireless networks for communication can be located in the references. [31-36]. Standard devices with transceivers, protocol stacks, and microcontrollers are known as Internet of Things objects.

Full automation may be achieved by facilitating connectivity between IoT devices and other devices, as well as external entities such as people [37]. Integrating smart grids is reliant on the IoT. IoT technology is used by the smart grid to improve its reliability, processing, disaster recovery, and self-healing capabilities. The incorporation of the IoT into the smart grid might potentially promote the use of intelligent meters, sensors, terminals, and other communication equipment. The IoT in the smart grid encompasses the tasks of monitoring the state of devices, gathering data, managing the whole smart grid, and guaranteeing security and safety [38].

3.1 Applications

3.1.1 IoT in Power Generation

Figure 6 illustrates the many applications of the smart grid in the IoT domain. The primary development of the IoT is in the acquisition of data, encompassing the acquisition of locations, essential smart equipment, and data about their distinctive alterations via sensors and instantaneous access. With the continuous advancement of IoT technology, there is a corresponding improvement in its theoretical system, including network architecture, operational mechanism, and transfer protocol. The primary objective of the IoT network function in the smart grid is to facilitate the collection, transfer, and analysis of information [39-40]. IoT technology is used throughout the generation stage to monitor the energy generation in many types of power plants. The system monitors the energy storage, gas emissions, and energy consumption of power plants. In parallel with the electrical grid, the identification and organization of manufacturing equipment for power plants are conducted. In instances of device breakdown or environmental fluctuations, judgments will be predicated upon the data gathered by an IoT collector. The power plant production monitoring system will be utilized to send precise advance notifications and reports to pertinent personnel for power forecasting, distributed power plant monitoring, coal monitoring, gas emission monitoring, energy consumption monitoring, energy storage monitoring, and factory pollutant monitoring. IoT technology allows for the monitoring of wide, panoramic, real-time, comprehensive, reliable, and trustworthy status information [39].

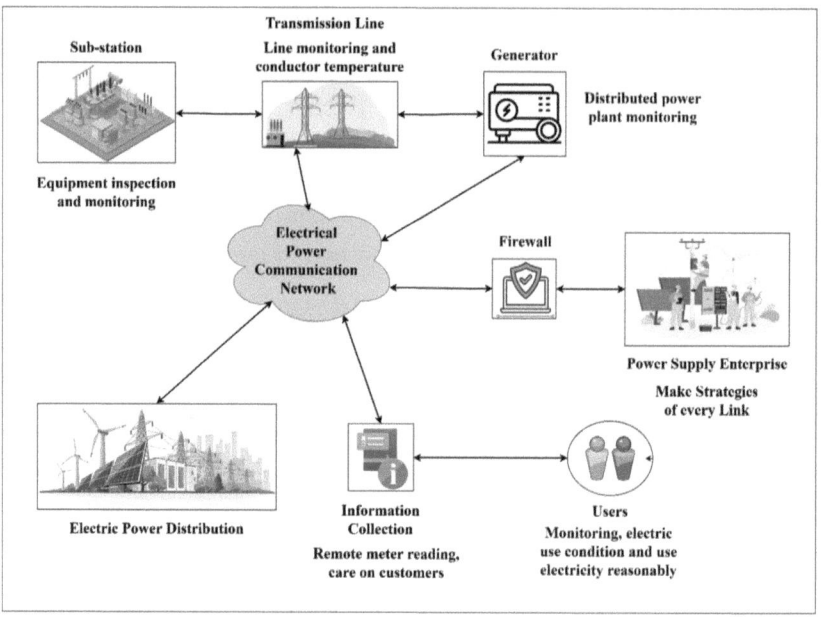

Figure 6 Applications of the smart grid in the IoT domain- "Author's own work"

3.1.2 IoT in Transmission

The transmission section shields the transmission lines from environmental factors including weather conditions such as meteorological climate, snowfall, temperature, and fog. Sensors placed in various locations may detect and monitor the high-voltage electrical components, mechanical status, environmental state, and operating conditions of the tower. For identifying and rectifying issues in the transmission lines, wireless broadband communication technologies are used. Under some circumstances, it utilizes a blend of communication networks to carry out the tasks of data handling, transmission, and valuation [39].

3.1.3 IoT in Substation

IoT supervises the functioning of substation machinery and ensures the environmental safety of the equipment during operation. Real-time monitoring of regional power distribution and consumption is possible with the help of this IoT technology, which is used by operators at substations, grid operations, and maintenance [39].

3.1.4 IoT in Distribution, Utilization, and Dispatch

IoT is used in power distribution automation, consumption data gathering, electrical load management, AMI, smart home technology, and SCADA in these areas. The IoT allows for two-way interactive services including smart power consumption, data gathering, home automation, and efficient family energy control, connection to decentralized power sources, and electric car charging and discharging. The use of IoT in smart meters for monitor different metrics, enable intelligent power usage, ensure network compatibility, and oversee power demand and energy efficiency [40].

3.1.5 IoT in Smart Metering

IoT plays a crucial role to generate energy, for communication, and for distribution, with the help of smart metering being a key component of IoT's use in smart grids. Meters may transmit data to ESPs via suitable interfaces utilizing IoT technologies. Regularly incorporating IoT technology into smart grids allows for increased data monitoring. Consequently, the likelihood of prompt initiation of crucial repairs in the event of malfunctions will increase. Integrating IoT into smart metering systems enhances the AMI by introducing intelligence and enhancing scalability [41].

4. Introduction to Edge Computing

4.1 Edge computing and its fundamental principles

The quantity of smart devices connected to the Internet has increased as a result of the 'Internet of Things' explosive growth. This has led to problems with typical cloud computing approaches, including insufficient security, inadequate privacy, limited bandwidth, and sluggish reaction times. A new computer paradigm called "edge" has been created to address these concerns. Moving some processing and storage capacity closer to the data source and away from the main data centre is known as EC [42]. Unprocessed data in cloud computing is typically examined near to its source, at the network edge, as opposed to being forwarded to the central cloud server for examination. The only results of edge computing operations that are sent directly to the central cloud server for evaluation and potential human intervention are forecasts for equipment repair and real-time business analytics. According to the authors' outline of Edge Computing, the cloud service is represented by the Edge Computing downlink data, the Edge Computing edge represents the computing and network resources between the data source and the Cloud Computing centre, and the Edge Computing uplink data displays the Internet of Things. US professor Satya Narayanan of Carnegie Mellon University claims that Edge Computing is a unique computing paradigm that involves putting processing and storage resources closer to mobile devices [44]. Processing is done by Edge Computing at the edge of the network. It highlights the importance of being near the user and the data source. It is instantaneous, dependable, and quicker. This paradigm may address issues like excessive energy consumption in cloud computing, network bandwidth constraints, latency, and increased expenses of cloud infrastructure [45]. Enterprise computing can meet the essential needs of the IT sector in optimizing data, establishing strong connections, monitoring applications, enabling real-time business operations, and ensuring privacy and security.

4.2 Important Features of Edge Computing [43]:

(i) **Computing and Networking**: By moving complex IT and network infrastructures to the edge of the network, edge computing makes it possible to process and store data close to the point of production.

(ii) **Storage**: In order to avoid obstructions and network problems, processing and storage devices are positioned at the base station close to end devices in the edge computing architecture. By improving QoS and QoE for end users and cutting down on data transmission delays, this could significantly increase the success of Smart Grid implementation.

(iii) **Data Management**: The centralised data management architecture of cloud computing is unable to keep up with the rapid data production in Smart Grids. A decentralised data management model's applicability has been the subject of several recent research.

4.3. Benefits of Edge Computing [15]

Stringent requirements in the complex and diverse Smart Grid environment exceed the capabilities of current cloud-based infrastructures. Edge computing has several advantages, making it a great platform for meeting Smart Grid needs effectively.

These benefits are covered in the sections that follow:

i **Reduced Latency**: Edge computing is advantageous for applications sensitive to latency since it focuses on minimizing data transmission delays and simplifying network architecture. [20].

ii **Ease of data processing**: Edge Computing's closeness to data sources allows for analysis and extraction of valuable insights from "big data." Given the anticipated rapid growth in the deployment of smart meters in Smart Grids, Edge Computing may enhance the management and analysis of data from these devices more effectively.

iii **Awareness of Location**: Edge Computing may execute computational tasks on data depending on its geographical location, which sets it apart from Cloud Computing. We can achieve this services without the use of Cloud Computing. Edge Computing gives better services for location awareness then Cloud Computing, which will improve Wide-Area Situational Awareness (WASA) performance in Smart Grids.

iv **Load balancing**: The resources in the mobile cloud network, situated in the network's periphery, provide diverse processing and storage capabilities. It is crucial to distribute the workload evenly across these resources while taking into account the various needs of users. Implementing load balancing on cloud services enhances dependability, availability, decreases response time, and boosts efficiency. [46] an overview of load-balancing techniques for mobile cloud services. The approaches rely on geographical area [47], mixed integer nonlinear programming [48], differential evolution [49], partitioning theory [50], and collaboration [51].

5. Integration of EC in Smart Grids

5.1 Edge computing's contribution to improving IoT device capabilities in smart grids

By utilising smart appliances, RESs, and smart metres, the Smart Grid is a pioneering technology that is revolutionising traditional networks, slashing utility bills, and stopping global warming. The detection, processing, and sharing of information has been extensively facilitated by the IoT-enabled smart grid. Conventional cloud computing is inadequate for IoT data processing due to the geographical distance of cloud servers, requiring multi-hop connection. Unacceptable transmission latency occurs in certain applications that are real-time. Unprocessed data is sent by IoT devices to cloud servers, which puts a significant strain on the communication network. As a result, reaction time and latency are no longer dependable. If raw data from IoT devices containing private or sensitive information is delivered straight to the public cloud, other parties may access it, leading to confidentiality and safety concerns. In order to resolve these problems, Edge computing manages the Internet of Things' data processing. For real-time applications, error correction reduces latency and network burden. Edge computing is seen as a beneficial strategy for addressing the limitations cloud computing within the intelligent grid by offering storage capacity and high-level processing at the edge of the network [52].

5.2 How edge computing allows real-time data processing, analysis, and decision-making at the network edge?

Edge Computing is adaptable for using computer resources throughout the continuum from devices to cloud resources. Community applications are programs capable of efficiently using and allocating computing resources across a range of systems. A community of intelligent agents for Smart Grid services and operations could be created with Edge Computing. The power transmission network, the power distribution network, or both acting in tandem can all contribute to the development of the community. Acquiring computing resources is not the same as creating community agents. Collaboration, negotiation, and compromise are essential within a society to achieve various goals with varying time frames and geographical scopes [53]. Popular examples of community resource development inside smart grids are micro-grids and virtual power plants (VPPs). (Smart Grid s). To respond rapidly to emergencies, for these systems to function, system inertia and transient stability must be provided fully dispersed at a sub-second level. At the regional level, independent management of the voltage control, frequency, and power balance services is necessary. In a regional cooperative approach, energy storage utilisation and cost optimisation are optimised down to the micron level. It might be necessary to make grid-connected decisions at the quarter-hour level globally, together with economic bidding optimisation. Based on the requirements of the applications and the characteristics of the computational resources available in the community, Edge Computing may dynamically optimise the distribution of computing resources. This method differs from the conventional multi-agent system in that it incorporates concurrent frameworks for competition, collaboration, and supervision. One illustration of this is the hybrid cloud-edge analytical technique, which is frequently employed in numerous research and effectively distributes compute tasks across Edge Computing nodes and the cloud. The development of a citywide energy management system makes use of Edge Computing infrastructure. Each edge node is transformed into an edge DRL agent by deep reinforcement learning (DRL), while the cloud is converted into the cloud DRL agent. Multiple agents work together to collaboratively carry out the training and inference process. The study described in reference [54] utilizes a cloud-edge computing architecture with three layers to improve energy management. The power network's structure is changed in order to do this while taking the dynamic thermal line rating (DLR) constraint into consideration. Benders cuts are generated using Edge Computing resources, and the cloud is chosen as the controller. The use of a remote cloud computing platform and a local DSP chip at the edge is the foundation of the dynamic economic dispatch paradigm proposed by [55]. Decision-making in real time is aided by Digital Signal Processing(DSP) chips, while calculations are performed offline by the remote cloud.

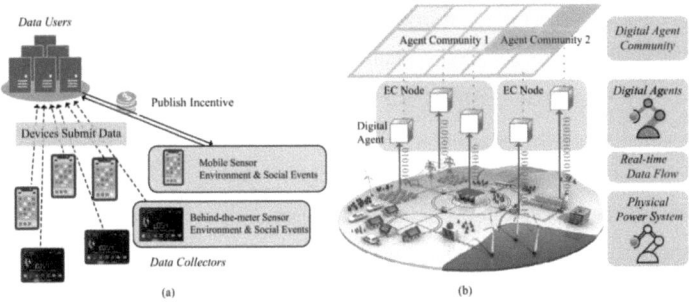

Figure 7 (a) Crowd-sensing (b) EC-based digital agent simulation[77]

Because it gathers and compiles data, the sensor community—along with the electrical agent community—is crucial to the Smart Grid. The traditional data collecting strategy involves sampling data at regular intervals and updating it compulsorily. However, the growing requirement for more data in the electrical distribution network may present difficulties for this established regulation. Devices that collect data are owned by multiple parties. They can be reluctant to give their sensor data. To encourage the sharing of data, effective incentives are needed [56]. Furthermore, data gathered from various devices may exhibit varying values depending on the application context. The significance of the data must be assessed by operators and service providers, who should then devote more processing and transmission resources to the more important data. The well-studied application of crowd-sensing with Edge Computing has been suggested as a remedy for these issues [57]. In crowd sensing, the sensors are known as data workers and are paid for gathering important data. Figure 7 shows the edge computing in crowd-sensing involves identifying new workers and sending alerts for data collection and gathering needs. By documenting the standing of data workers, which measures the dependability of the data they supply, Edge Computing might determine the significance of sensors [58]. Furthermore, rather than constantly gathering extensive data, Edge Computing may provide specific data collection requests that are relevant to smart grid activities and enterprises, thereby reducing a rise in the flow of data.

The cyber communities that are created with Edge Computing have the potential to develop into a digital twin system that would support Smart Grids in the networks that handle distribution and transmission of power. Historically, Computer simulations have been used by power grid operators that use programmed analytic solutions for synchronous generator equipment to forecast system behaviours. The accuracy of conventional simulations is being undermined by the increasing complexity of users and technology. Through thought, Edge computing may replicate the Smart Grid devices inside its region using data while preserving intricate nuances. Additionally, Edge Computing has the ability to digitally reproduce the states and activities within the same virtual depiction of a particular item or person. Subsequently, the simulation involving hardware and human-in-the-loop could be executed with Edge Computing resources. Operatives may use Edge Computing resources to simulate grid components while testing a dispatch/schedule strategy. Service organizations may simulate grid customers' bargaining behaviours using Edge Computing to evaluate the impact of a demand response scheme. The digital twin platform maintenance is the responsibility of the platform owner, while testing initiatives should be funded by the platform users. The physical system is translated into a geo-distributed, agent-based, parallel digital equivalent. Real-time data connects the virtual and physical models. In Smart Grid, simulations are dynamic; digital models could change instantly in response to changes in their physical counterparts. This digital copy kept on Edge Computing resources can be used for simulations that yield results exactly like those of the real network. Elastic updating strategies or alternative communication technologies, such as 5G, may be utilised in the digital twin system to save communication overhead. To improve the twin system's performance, Optimising the allocation and scheduling of computational resources is necessary. This idea originated with the satellite/aviation industry [59].

6. Challenges and Open Issues

Smart grids have seen a strong application of edge computing and Internet of Things technology in recent years. Smart grid applications are still in their infancy, though. Smart grid development will only be forced if numerous difficult issues are resolved in the near future. Figure 8 provides the following summary of these issues:

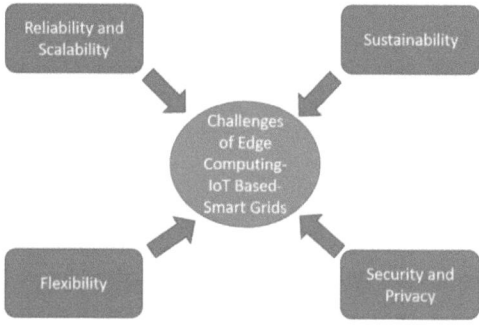

Figure 8 Challenges of EC-IoT Based Smart Grids- "Author's own work"

6.1 Scalability and Reliability

Smart Grids will gain popularity in the IoT-5G era, that will result in an increase in sensors, actuators, and other clever Internet of things devices. Data traffic will therefore grow quickly, placing strain on backbone bandwidth and causing significant latency. Edge computing offers a way to tackle these difficult issues. But in order to create a scalable and trustworthy. The multitude of smart Internet of Things devices, the diversity of network environments, power sources, and users are all factors that need to be taken into account while constructing edge computing infrastructure. [62]. By including new coverage sites and secure technologies, the Electrical Vehicle infrastructure may become more resilient and dependable [63]. But the primary difficulties with are scalability and reliability. Because of the high degree of dynamic nature of smart grids and the security vulnerabilities in hardware and software, edge computing is used in the infrastructure of these systems.

6.2. Sustainability

One major extra challenge in designing Smart Grid infrastructure based on Edge Computing is sustainability. The authors of [64] have provided a distinct sustainable development goals architecture (SDGs) that is based on four indicators. This architecture states that factors related to energy, materials, finances, and labour are necessary for Smart Grids to be sustainable. This subject also considers the development of energy-efficient technology and the use of renewable resources in an effort to reduce the world's carbon footprint. The use of renewable energy sources [65], smart energy harvesting management systems [66], and energy-efficient systems [67] are the three primary connected features of Edge Computing-based Smart Grid sustainability. The sustainability of Smart Grid systems can be implemented by balancing demand, enforcing computational resource allocation methods, and offloading to optimise the system, all of which rely on Edge Computing and IoT.

6.4 Security and Privacy

In the age of IoT, security and privacy are the biggest issues for Smart Grid. Cybersecurity and physical security are the two primary facets of security problems in Edge Computing -IoT-based Smart Grids. These concerns concern data security, networks, Internet of Things (IoT) devices, authentication techniques, and computing infrastructure resistance to attacks [68], [69]. The privacy issues specify guidelines for establishing and offering different degrees of protection. Privacy places restrictions on who is authorised to access data. A number of tools and technologies, including distributed systems, virtualization, deep learning, and D2D communications, are used in an Edge Computing–IoT-based Smart Grid. Edge nodes operate in a dispersed manner. As such, edge server security and privacy issues are pressing and will likely be resolved quickly. Robust cryptographic methods, including block chain [70] and completely homomorphic encryption [71], have been developed recently to improve data privacy and thwart attacks.

6.3 Flexibility

One of the key problems of Edge Computing -based Smart Grids is flexibility, which is achieved by allocating system resources optimally [72], delivering adaptable services in accordance with dynamic demand, and meeting QoS requirements [73]. The system must anticipate end-user requests, adapt to service providers' capabilities, and take into account real-time system elements in order to achieve genuine flexibility in an Edge Computing -based Smart Grid. This covers the distribution and release of computing resources, such as memory, bandwidth, and processing capacity. In order to maximise the transmission of sensor data, [74] has created dual prediction algorithms.

The authors of [75] provide an autonomous resource provisioning architecture that leverages machine learning and computing approaches. One can apply auto-scaling methods in a hybrid, vertical, or horizontal fashion. While resource allocation within a node can be resized, resource allocation across nodes in a cluster can only be resized using horizontal solutions. [76] provides an example of a sophisticated hybrid autonomic resource provisioning framework with both vertical and horizontal components.

7. Future Directions and Conclusion

Smart Grid technology is seen as a possible remedy for the issues encountered by conventional power networks, such as energy inefficiency, security concerns, and increasing energy use. Flexible Load Distribution for Adaptive Virtual Machine Reorganisation Using Vertical and Horizontal Scaling. Edge computing offers computational and storage resources in close proximity to the network's edge, thereby resolving this issue. This chapter presents a framework for an edge computing Internet of things system that offers increased energy management, cost-effective and efficient operation, and dependable bidirectional resource and data flow. Advancements in these systems will result in improved energy management, enhanced efficiency, and less energy wastage, which will be advantageous for consumers and the environment. The worldwide need for renewable energy necessitates novel and advanced technologies. By using Analytics at the Edge, Smart Grid power utilities may more effectively manage personnel and resources, predict and prevent problems in real time, and improve grid security, dependability, and optimisation. In order to achieve their mission of delivering dependability, affordability, and sustainability, Smart Grid power utilities may extract helpful, actionable insights from operational data by combining cutting-edge Edge Computing and IoT technology with a modern architecture [23].

8. References

[1] R. A. Aleksandrovich and K. T. Arturovich, "Survey of IoT application layer protocols," Jan. 08, 2024. doi: 10.5281/zenodo.10471669.

[2] S. N. H. Shah, "IoT Enabled Smart Grid Integration with Edge Computing Method," in *2023 International Conference on Communication, Computing and Digital Systems (C-CODE)*, May 2023, pp. 1–6. doi: 10.1109/C-CODE58145.2023.10139871.

[3] L. Tan and N. Wang, "Future internet: The Internet of Things," in *2010 3rd International Conference on Advanced Computer Theory and Engineering(ICACTE)*, Aug. 2010, pp. V5-376-V5-380. doi: 10.1109/ICACTE.2010.5579543.

[4] P. Radanliev, D. De Roure, R. Nicolescu, M. Huth, and O. Santos, "Artificial Intelligence and the Internet of Things in Industry 4.0," *CCF Trans. Pervasive Comput. Interact.*, vol. 3, no. 3, pp. 329–338, Sep. 2021, doi: 10.1007/s42486-021-00057-3.

[5] K. Ystgaard *et al.*, "Review of the theory, principles, and design requirements of human-centric Internet of Things (IoT)," *J. Ambient Intell. Humaniz. Comput.*, vol. 14, pp. 1–33, Feb. 2023, doi: 10.1007/s12652-023-04539-3.

[6] "(PDF) The Internet of Things (IoT) and its impact on individual privacy: An Australian perspective." Accessed: Feb. 26, 2024. [Online]. Available: https://www.researchgate.net/publication/288918372_The_Internet_of_Things_IoT_and_its_i mpact_on_individual_privacy_An_Australian_perspective

[7] M. Ammar, G. Russello, and B. Crispo, "Internet of Things: A survey on the security of IoT frameworks," *J. Inf. Secur. Appl.*, vol. 38, pp. 8–27, Feb. 2018, doi: 10.1016/j.jisa.2017.11.002.

[8]   B. Guo, D. Zhang, Z. Wang, Z. Yu, and X. Zhou, "Opportunistic IoT: Exploring the harmonious interaction between human and the internet of things," *J. Netw. Comput. Appl.*, vol. 36, no. 6, pp. 1531–1539, Nov. 2013, doi: 10.1016/j.jnca.2012.12.028.

[9]   Rani and A. Malik, "A social relationship-based energy efficient routing scheme for Opportunistic Internet of Things," *ICT Express*, vol. 9, no. 4, pp. 697–705, Aug. 2023, doi: 10.1016/j.icte.2022.10.002.

[10]   V.-V. Fireteanu, "Agile Methodology Advantages when delivering Internet of Things projects," Jun. 2020, pp. 1–5. doi: 10.1109/ECAI50035.2020.9223172.

[11]   X. Mu and M. F. Antwi-Afari, "The applications of Internet of Things (IoT) in industrial management: a science mapping review," *Int. J. Prod. Res.*, vol. 62, no. 5, pp. 1928–1952, Mar. 2024, doi: 10.1080/00207543.2023.2290229.

[12]   W. Meng, R. Ma, and H.-H. Chen, "Smart grid neighborhood area networks: a survey," *IEEE Netw.*, vol. 28, no. 1, pp. 24–32, Jan. 2014, doi: 10.1109/MNET.2014.6724103.

[13]   F. Samie, L. Bauer, and J. Henkel, "IoT technologies for embedded computing: A survey," in *2016 International Conference on Hardware/Software Codesign and System Synthesis (CODES+ISSS)*, Oct. 2016, pp. 1–10. Accessed: Feb. 26, 2024. [Online]. Available: https://ieeexplore.ieee.org/abstract/document/7750968

[14]   "A Vision of IoT: Applications, Challenges, and Opportunities With China Perspective | IEEE Journals & Magazine | IEEE Xplore." Accessed: Feb. 26, 2024. [Online]. Available: https://ieeexplore.ieee.org/document/6851114

[15]   S. Chen *et al.*, "Internet of Things Based Smart Grids Supported by Intelligent Edge Computing," *IEEE Access*, vol. 7, pp. 74089–74102, 2019, doi: 10.1109/ACCESS.2019.2920488.

[16]   H. Abd ul Muqeet, H. M. Munir, A. Ahmad, I. A. Sajjad, G.-J. Jiang, and H.-X. Chen, "Optimal Operation of the Campus Microgrid considering the Resource Uncertainty and Demand Response Schemes," *Math. Probl. Eng.*, vol. 2021, p. e5569701, May 2021, doi: 10.1155/2021/5569701.

[17]   A. Habib, H. Anam, W. Anwaar, H. Afaq, Y. Amin, and H. Tenhunen, "Internet-of-things based smart tracking," in *2017 International Conference on Communication, Computing and Digital Systems (C-CODE)*, Mar. 2017, pp. 44–47. doi: 10.1109/C-CODE.2017.7918899.

[18]   M. Y. Mehmood *et al.*, "Edge Computing for IoT-Enabled Smart Grid," *Secur. Commun. Netw.*, vol. 2021, p. e5524025, Jul. 2021, doi: 10.1155/2021/5524025.

[19]   A. Basit, G. A. S. Sidhu, A. Mahmood, and F. Gao, "Efficient and Autonomous Energy Management Techniques for the Future Smart Homes," *IEEE Trans. Smart Grid*, vol. 8, no. 2, pp. 917–926, Mar. 2017, doi: 10.1109/TSG.2015.2504560.

[20]   "Collaborative service oriented smart grid using the Internet of Things | IEEE Conference Publication | IEEE Xplore." Accessed: Feb. 26, 2024. [Online]. Available: https://ieeexplore.ieee.org/abstract/document/7754459

[21]   "(PDF) A New Automatic Method for Control Chart Patterns Recognition Based on ConvNet and Harris Hawks Meta Heuristic Optimization Algorithm." Accessed: Feb. 26, 2024. [Online]. Available: https://www.researchgate.net/publication/336268733_A_New_Automatic_Method_for_Control_Chart_Patterns_Recognition_Based_on_ConvNet_and_Harris_Hawks_Meta_Heuristic_Optimization_Algorithm

[22]   J. Arshad *et al.*, "Intelligent greenhouse monitoring and control scheme: An arrangement of Sensors, Raspberry Pi based Embedded System and IoT platform," *Indian J. Sci. Technol.*, vol. 13, pp. 2811–2822, Jul. 2020, doi: 10.17485/IJST/v13i27.311.

[23]   J. Guo, H. Zheng, B. Li, and G.-Z. Fu, "A Bayesian Approach for Degradation Analysis with Individual Differences," *IEEE Access*, vol. 7, pp. 175033–175040, 2019, doi: 10.1109/ACCESS.2019.2955969.

[24] "Bayesian Hierarchical Model-Based Information Fusion for Degradation Analysis Considering Non-Competing Relationship - NASA/ADS." Accessed: Feb. 26, 2024. [Online]. Available: https://ui.adsabs.harvard.edu/abs/2019IEEEA...7q5222G/abstract

[25] F. Ye, Y. Qian, R. Hu, and S. Das, "Reliable Energy-Efficient Uplink Transmission for Neighborhood Area Networks in Smart Grid," *IEEE Trans. Smart Grid*, vol. 6, no. 5, pp. 2179–2188, Sep. 2015, doi: 10.1109/TSG.2015.2392130.

[26] Y. Liu, C. Yuen, Y. Zhang, and S. Xie, "Queuing-Based Energy Consumption Management for Heterogeneous Residential Demands in Smart Grid," *IEEE Trans. Smart Grid*, vol. 7, pp. 1–1, Jun. 2015, doi: 10.1109/TSG.2015.2432571.

[27] "(PDF) Three-Party Energy Management With Distributed Energy Resources in Smart Grid." Accessed: Feb. 26, 2024. [Online]. Available: https://www.researchgate.net/publication/263352321_Three-Party_Energy_Management_With_Distributed_Energy_Resources_in_Smart_Grid

[28] Y. Liu, M. Pan, Y. Zhang, and S. Xie, "SD-MAC: Spectrum Database-Driven MAC Protocol for Cognitive Machine-to-Machine Networks," *IEEE Trans. Veh. Technol.*, vol. 66, pp. 1–1, Jan. 2016, doi: 10.1109/TVT.2016.2555084.

[29] S. Bera, S. Misra, and J. J. P. C. Rodrigues, "Cloud Computing Applications for Smart Grid: A Survey," *IEEE Trans. Parallel Distrib. Syst.*, vol. 26, no. 5, pp. 1477–1494, May 2015, doi: 10.1109/TPDS.2014.2321378.

[30] S. Patra, B. Dash, T. Pandey, B. Pattanayak, A. Tripathy, and U. De, "Energy-Efficient Task Offloading for Edge Computing-Based Smart Grid Networks Using Human Urbanization," Jan. 2024. doi: 10.1109/ICSCNA58489.2023.10370039.

[31] F. Liu *et al.*, "NIST Cloud Computing Reference Architecture," *NIST*, Sep. 2011, Accessed: Feb. 26, 2024. [Online]. Available: https://www.nist.gov/publications/nist-cloud-computing-reference-architecture

[32] S. Behera, N. Panda, U. C. De, B. B. Dash, B. Dash, and S. S. Patra, "A task offloading scheme with Queue Dependent VM in fog Center," in *2023 6th International Conference on Information Systems and Computer Networks (ISCON)*, IEEE, 2023, pp. 1–5. Accessed: Feb. 26, 2024. [Online]. Available: https://ieeexplore.ieee.org/abstract/document/10112106/

[33] B. B. Dash, R. Satapathy, and S. S. Patra, "Energy Efficient SDN-assisted Routing Scheme in Cloud Data Center," in *2023 2nd International Conference on Vision Towards Emerging Trends in Communication and Networking Technologies (ViTECoN)*, May 2023, pp. 1–5. doi: 10.1109/ViTECoN58111.2023.10157706.

[34] S. E. Collier, "The Emerging Enernet: Convergence of the Smart Grid with the Internet of Things," *IEEE Ind. Appl. Mag.*, vol. 23, no. 2, pp. 12–16, Mar. 2017, doi: 10.1109/MIAS.2016.2600737.

[35] R. Deng, Z. Yang, M.-Y. Chow, and J. Chen, "A Survey on Demand Response in Smart Grids: Mathematical Models and Approaches," *IEEE Trans. Ind. Inform.*, vol. 11, no. 3, pp. 570–582, Jun. 2015, doi: 10.1109/TII.2015.2414719.

[36] "Smart Grid Communication: Its Challenges and Opportunities | IEEE Journals & Magazine | IEEE Xplore." Accessed: Feb. 26, 2024. [Online]. Available: https://ieeexplore.ieee.org/document/6451177

[37] E. Yaacoub and A. Abu-Dayya, "Automatic meter reading in the smart grid using contention based random access over the free cellular spectrum," *Comput. Netw.*, vol. 59, pp. 171–183, Feb. 2014, doi: 10.1016/j.bjp.2013.10.009.

[38] "World electricity generation by energy source 2050," Statista. Accessed: Feb. 26, 2024. [Online]. Available: https://www.statista.com/statistics/238610/projected-world-electricity-generation-by-energy-source/

[39] Q. Minh, V.-H. Nguyen, Q. Vu Khanh, L. Ngoc, A. Chehri, and G. Jeon, "Edge Computing for IoT-Enabled Smart Grid: The Future of Energy," *Energies*, vol. 15, p. 6140, Aug. 2022, doi: 10.3390/en15176140.

[40] Y. Saleem, N. Crespi, M. H. Rehmani, and R. Copeland, "Internet of Things-Aided Smart Grid: Technologies, Architectures, Applications, Prototypes, and Future Research Directions," *IEEE Access*, vol. 7, pp. 62962–63003, 2019, doi: 10.1109/ACCESS.2019.2913984.

[41] s. M. A. A. Abir, A. Anwar, J. Choi, and A. S. M. Kayes, "IoT-Enabled Smart Energy Grid: Applications and Challenges," *IEEE Access*, vol. PP, pp. 1–1, Mar. 2021, doi: 10.1109/ACCESS.2021.3067331.

[42] "Energy-Efficient Information and Communication Infrastructures in the Smart Grid: A Survey on Interactions and Open Issues | IEEE Journals & Magazine | IEEE Xplore." Accessed: Feb. 26, 2024. [Online]. Available: https://ieeexplore.ieee.org/document/6861946

[43] A. Čolaković and M. Hadžialić, "Internet of Things (IoT): A review of enabling technologies, challenges, and open research issues," *Comput. Netw.*, vol. 144, pp. 17–39, Oct. 2018, doi: 10.1016/j.comnet.2018.07.017.

[44] M. Satyanarayanan, "The Emergence of Edge Computing," *Computer*, vol. 50, no. 1, pp. 30–39, Jan. 2017, doi: 10.1109/MC.2017.9.

[45] K. Cao, Y. Liu, G. Meng, and Q. Sun, "An Overview on Edge Computing Research," *IEEE Access*, vol. 8, pp. 85714–85728, 2020, doi: 10.1109/ACCESS.2020.2991734.

[46] E. Jafarnejad Ghomi, A. Masoud Rahmani, and N. Nasih Qader, "Load-balancing algorithms in cloud computing: A survey," *J. Netw. Comput. Appl.*, vol. 88, pp. 50–71, Jun. 2017, doi: 10.1016/j.jnca.2017.04.007.

[47] H. Wu, L. Chen, C. Shen, W. Wen, and J. Xu, "Online Geographical Load Balancing for Energy-Harvesting Mobile Edge Computing," *2018 IEEE Int. Conf. Commun. ICC*, pp. 1–6, May 2018, doi: 10.1109/ICC.2018.8422299.

[48] Y. Dai, D. Xu, S. Maharjan, and Y. Zhang, "Joint Load Balancing and Offloading in Vehicular Edge Computing and Networks," *IEEE Internet Things J.*, vol. PP, pp. 1–1, Oct. 2018, doi: 10.1109/JIOT.2018.2876298.

[49] L. Yang, H. Yao, J. Wang, C. Jiang, A. Benslimane, and Y. Liu, "Multi-UAV Enabled Load-Balance Mobile Edge Computing for IoT Networks," *IEEE Internet Things J.*, vol. PP, Feb. 2020, doi: 10.1109/JIOT.2020.2971645.

[50] S. Ningning, G. Chao, A. Xingshuo, and Z. Qiang, "Fog computing dynamic load balancing mechanism based on graph repartitioning," *China Commun.*, vol. 13, no. 3, pp. 156–164, Mar. 2016, doi: 10.1109/CC.2016.7445510.

[51] R. Beraldi, A. Mtibaa, and H. Alnuweiri, "Cooperative load balancing scheme for edge computing resources," in *2017 Second International Conference on Fog and Mobile Edge Computing (FMEC)*, May 2017, pp. 94–100. doi: 10.1109/FMEC.2017.7946414.

[52] T. X. Tran, A. Hajisami, P. Pandey, and D. Pompili, "Collaborative Mobile Edge Computing in 5G Networks: New Paradigms, Scenarios, and Challenges," *IEEE Commun. Mag.*, vol. 55, no. 4, pp. 54–61, Apr. 2017, doi: 10.1109/MCOM.2017.1600863.

[53] "Multi-Agent Systems for Power Engineering Applications—Part I: Concepts, Approaches, and Technical Challenges | IEEE Journals & Magazine | IEEE Xplore." Accessed: Feb. 27, 2024. [Online]. Available: https://ieeexplore.ieee.org/document/4349106

[54] M. Dabbaghjamanesh, A. Kavousi-Fard, and Z. Y. Dong, "A Novel Distributed Cloud-Fog Based Framework for Energy Management of Networked Microgrids," *IEEE Trans. Power Syst.*, vol. 35, no. 4, pp. 2847–2862, Jul. 2020, doi: 10.1109/TPWRS.2019.2957704.

[55] S. Wang, X. Wang, and W. Wu, "Cloud Computing and Local Chip-Based Dynamic Economic Dispatch for Microgrids," *IEEE Trans. Smart Grid*, vol. 11, no. 5, pp. 3774–3784, Sep. 2020, doi: 10.1109/TSG.2020.2983556.

[56] G. Gao, M. Xiao, J. Wu, S. Zhang, L. Huang, and G. Xiao, "DPDT: A Differentially Private Crowd-Sensed Data Trading Mechanism," *IEEE Internet Things J.*, vol. 7, no. 1, pp. 751–762, Jan. 2020, doi: 10.1109/JIOT.2019.2944107.

[57] "Edge Computing Architecture for Mobile Crowdsensing | IEEE Journals & Magazine | IEEE Xplore." Accessed: Feb. 27, 2024. [Online]. Available: https://ieeexplore.ieee.org/document/8272334

[58] G. Zhu, D. Liu, Y. Du, C. You, J. Zhang, and K. Huang, "Toward an Intelligent Edge: Wireless Communication Meets Machine Learning," *IEEE Commun. Mag.*, vol. 58, no. 1, pp. 19–25, Jan. 2020, doi: 10.1109/MCOM.001.1900103.

[59] X. Zhang *et al.*, "Hardware-in-the-loop simulation system for space information networks," *J. Commun. Inf. Netw.*, vol. 2, no. 4, pp. 131–141, Dec. 2017, doi: 10.1007/s41650-017-0046-2.

[60] "Smart grid design for efficient and flexible power networks operation and control | IEEE Conference Publication | IEEE Xplore." Accessed: Mar. 06, 2024. [Online]. Available: https://ieeexplore.ieee.org/document/4840074

[61] "Recent advancement in smart grid technology: Future prospects in the electrical power network - ScienceDirect." Accessed: Mar. 06, 2024. [Online]. Available: https://www.sciencedirect.com/science/article/pii/S2090447920301064?via%3Dihub

[62] L. Dong, W. Wu, Q. Guo, M. N. Satpute, T. Znati, and D. Z. Du, "Reliability-Aware Offloading and Allocation in Multilevel Edge Computing System," *IEEE Transactions on Reliability*, vol. 70, no. 1, pp. 200–211, Mar. 2021, doi: 10.1109/TR.2019.2909279.

[63] K. Henzler, S. D. Maier, M. Jäger, and R. Horn, "SDG-Based Sustainability Assessment Methodology for Innovations in the Field of Urban Surfaces," *Sustainability*, vol. 12, no. 11, Art. no. 11, Jan. 2020, doi: 10.3390/su12114466.

[64] Z. Amjad *et al.*, "Towards Energy Efficient Smart Grids Using Bio-Inspired Scheduling Techniques," *IEEE Access*, vol. 8, pp. 158947–158960, 2020, doi: 10.1109/ACCESS.2020.3020027.

[65] S. Hu, X. Chen, W. Ni, X. Wang, and E. Hossain, "Modeling and Analysis of Energy Harvesting and Smart Grid-Powered Wireless Communication Networks: A Contemporary Survey," *IEEE Transactions on Green Communications and Networking*, vol. 4, no. 2, pp. 461–496, Jun. 2020, doi: 10.1109/TGCN.2020.2988270.

[66] M. B. Rasheed, M. A. Qureshi, N. Javaid, and T. Alquthami, "Dynamic Pricing Mechanism With the Integration of Renewable Energy Source in Smart Grid," *IEEE Access*, vol. 8, pp. 16876–16892, 2020, doi: 10.1109/ACCESS.2020.2967798.

[67] R.-F. Liao *et al.*, "Security Enhancement for Mobile Edge Computing Through Physical Layer Authentication," *IEEE Access*, vol. 7, pp. 116390–116401, 2019, doi: 10.1109/ACCESS.2019.2934122.

[68] L. Dias and T. A. Rizzetti, "A Review of Privacy-Preserving Aggregation Schemes for Smart Grid," *IEEE Latin America Transactions*, vol. 19, no. 7, pp. 1109–1120, Jul. 2021, doi: 10.1109/TLA.2021.9461839.

[69] Z. Zeng, M. Dong, W. Miao, M. Zhang, and H. Tang, "A Data-Driven Approach for Blockchain-Based Smart Grid System," *IEEE Access*, vol. 9, pp. 70061–70070, 2021, doi: 10.1109/ACCESS.2021.3076746.

[70] A. Mohammadali and M. S. Haghighi, "A Privacy-Preserving Homomorphic Scheme With Multiple Dimensions and Fault Tolerance for Metering Data Aggregation in Smart Grid," *IEEE Transactions on Smart Grid*, vol. 12, no. 6, pp. 5212–5220, Nov. 2021, doi: 10.1109/TSG.2021.3049222.

[71] D. Wang, M. Chen, and W. Wang, "Distributed Extremum Seeking for Optimal Resource Allocation and Its Application to Economic Dispatch in Smart Grids," *IEEE Transactions on Neural Networks and Learning Systems*, vol. 30, no. 10, pp. 3161–3171, Oct. 2019, doi: 10.1109/TNNLS.2018.2890115.

[72] S. Misra, A. Mondal, P. V. S. Kumar, and S. K. Pal, "SEED: QoS-Aware Sustainable Energy Distribution in Smart Grid," *IEEE Transactions on Sustainable Computing*, vol. 7, no. 1, pp. 211–220, Jan. 2022, doi: 10.1109/TSUSC.2021.3049132.

[73] G. M. Dias, B. Bellalta, and S. Oechsner, "The impact of dual prediction schemes on the reduction of the number of transmissions in sensor networks," *Computer Communications*, vol. 112, pp. 58–72, Nov. 2017, doi: 10.1016/j.comcom.2017.08.002.

[74] M. Ghobaei-Arani, S. Jabbehdari, and M. A. Pourmina, "An autonomic resource provisioning approach for service-based cloud applications: A hybrid approach," *Future Generation Computer Systems*, vol. 78, pp. 191–210, Jan. 2018, doi: 10.1016/j.future.2017.02.022.

[75] N. Cruz Coulson, S. Sotiriadis, and N. Bessis, "Adaptive Microservice Scaling for Elastic Applications," *IEEE Internet of Things Journal*, vol. 7, no. 5, pp. 4195–4202, May 2020, doi: 10.1109/JIOT.2020.2964405.

[76] S. Sotiriadis, N. Bessis, C. Amza, and R. Buyya, "Elastic Load Balancing for Dynamic Virtual Machine Reconfiguration Based on Vertical and Horizontal Scaling," *IEEE Transactions on Services Computing*, vol. 12, no. 2, pp. 319–334, Mar. 2019, doi: 10.1109/TSC.2016.2634024.

[77] C. Feng, Y. Wang, Q. Chen, Y. Ding, G. Strbac, and C. Kang, "Smart grid encounters edge computing: opportunities and applications," *Advances in Applied Energy*, vol. 1, p. 100006, Feb. 2021, doi: 10.1016/j.adapen.2020.100006.